Prai

Once again
welcome, but dares men to enter the truth
of all weather that is Woman. These poems
are the goal of many but the achievement of
one. Lopez has the ability to describe
wrath and loss as a pretty dream, a scar as
a "blood star," and the anatomy that is
woman as a galaxy. She has a natural way of
inspiring the reader and reminding us the
work of writing matters.

~John S. Blake, poet, performer, youth activist,
and overall survivor

Breathtakingly tender, playful, and
generous one moment; sharp and
unapologetically brutal the next, these
poems transport the reader into the complex
landscape of feminine power with a dynamic
but inarguable force. Honest to the marrow,
Lopez never sugarcoats. And yet this work
rings with a sweetness nonetheless: the
kind it takes a warrior to earn. Lopez
knows what she's fighting for, what has
been lost, and where to attack to set the
wheels of justice in motion. Most
importantly, she has the teeth for it.

~Tatyana Brown, Editor of Tandem literary
journal and curator of San Francisco's premiere
poetry reading/slam The Lit Slam

Cunt.Bomb.

a chapbook

Jessica Helen Lopez

Foreword

When I first laid my purdy little eyes on Igna Muscio's book, *Cunt – Decalaration of Independence*, I damn near exploded with happiness. The next thought I had was, "I am home." And truly, who wouldn't be at home within the velvety walls of the cunt, the embrace of the womb, and the blue-black ocean of true origin?

With voracious eyes, ears and tongue I lapped up Muscio's words. I drank from the modern fount of her fourth-wave feminism discourse. I had the same type of out-of-body experience earlier in my years when I first read Sandra Cisnero's, "Loose Woman." And again when a beloved professor gifted me Gloria Anzaldua's, "Borderlands." These precious jewels of epiphany continue to guide me as I uncover for myself women, gender-identified women and allies who advocate for equality, who fight against the oppression and pillage against women and of course who dive whole-heartedly into the vastness and mysterious complexity of unbridled sexuality.

Yes, I love the cunt. Yes, I have one. And yes, I will continue to use the word because it is not disparaging but rather has been wrangled into submission for hundreds of years; only to be used against women and girls as a tool for abuse and means of brutal capitulation. For those who recoil at the thought of the title of this humble chapbook, I invite you to sit and listen/read for a bit.

The poems included are but a small journey stitched together to create my life as a mother, daughter, sister, poet, and woman of color. Woman. Cunt.

Nadia Tolokannikova, oppositional artist and renegade member of Russian punk band Pussy Riot who was brutally incarcerated by the authoritarian patriarch of its legal system said, "We are persecuted but not forsaken. It's easy to humiliate and crush people who are open, but when I am weak, then I am strong."

Just like the cunt, with her commanding ability to create (or destroy) life, cyclically regenerate primordial blood, to give and take sexual pleasure as well as to be vulnerable against attackers; she is also a target for the greedy, the manipulative, the misogynist, and the rapist. The cunt is a bull's eye for those who want, need and must exploit it. Though, let us all remember, the cunt is absolutely and inextricably linked to the divine – a bomb stitched in trip wire, taut, ready and everlastingly strong.

Contents

Cunt.Bomb.

the c is as insidious
as a paper cut
as pleasurable as a paper boat—
if you happen to know how to fold
one and let it ride

the u of it lies between your legs
look down lovingly
lucky you if you happen to have one

pet it if you will
pet it as if it is the pet
rabbit your mother
never let you have

the cunt is absolutely
not a bomb
it will not hand-grenade explode
your skull open like a cantaloupe

brain matter writhing against
the wall behind your head

it will not shred your hands
to lace if you happen to finger
the trigger every now and now

the cunt *is*
most definitely
a bomb

you may strap it to your chest
and there it will reside like

your own personal rattlesnake

do not attempt to rob banks with it

Do however –

tell your boss that you own a cunt
(you have the receipt to prove it)
and watch how on the inside
he faints like little boy blue

Do however –

tell your teacher that you can spell cunt
that if you happen to extract letters
from the available alphabet
and arrange them in a certain fashion

this is what
you get:

C-U-N-T

the cunt is not a rude house guest
soiling the kitchen towels, sneaking
bacon scraps to your arthritic dog

the cunt is not a rapist
nor a necromancer

because Webster says it so
cunt is the most disparaging word
in the English language

it will make men
both want to fuck you

and bash your face in

because of this they are fire engine
red-faced
and embarrassed

because of this
you should wear it
like a good perfume on
the soft side of the wrists

which is to say the n
forces your tongue to the
top of your mouth
causing you to bare
your teeth ever slightly so

Nnnnn—

note that the t is the marvel of it all
tying everything up
in a neat and tidied corset
like a coin purse

or a straight jacket

Here are some fun things you too
can do with the word cunt –

Google it and it is insured
you will have hours of fun

hold it to the sunlight
like your favorite kaleidoscope

create a word search
in which every word is
the word cunt

reconcile the word cunt
by writing a poem no one
will ever publish

challenge yourself to define
the word cunt to your nine year-old
daughter

rack up a triple letter score
next time you scrabble

translate cunt *en espanol*
and impress your folks
with such tonguetastics as –

chucha
choncha
cucha
cuca

and the ever masculine version –

coño

there is nothing
more sensual than
a cunt who can wear a *tilde*
like a party dress

recall that the cunt
yields great power
which is to say

it will scare great many
a people

one last
recommendation

scrawl the word cunt
on one hundred and one
small pieces of white paper
each a small and distinct snowflake

insert into randomly selected books
located on the shelves of your
favorite library

walk away and wait
watch the fallout
for years and years and years
to come

the word cunt
will float
back down to earth
like confetti
or a deafening
ash

Feminism is a socialist, anti-family, political movement that encourages women to leave their husbands, kill their children, practice witchcraft, destroy capitalism and become lesbians.

-Pat Robertson, political sphincter

What the Womb Isn't

the womb isn't your cemetery
your fire escape, your sticks
and stones diatribe

it isn't empty swan song or slick-shoed
pole dance

it isn't without fire, without magnanimous
thunder roar nor the strength of eggshell
around embryo

it is all things physics
it is all things holy and unholy

the womb
the belly
the mound
the convex and concave
the body song
the abortion
the birth
the afterbirth
murmur congealed
purple and pulsating placenta

the womb isn't your political bastard
your 5 o' clock news
top story whore
ballot stuffer
wedge issue appetizer plate

the womb isn't
the womb isn't
the womb isn't
a third-rate quote

it is fire-spark
it is Corn Goddess
Tonatzin, eater
of the good filth
and maker of man
and woman

the water-rush of menses

it is the last blood kernel
protected by the husk.

A Poem for My Breasts

The striations are present. The puckered
zipper scars like trolley tracks. The
brown nipples my daughter never suckled.
One small cherry mark on the left tit that
I name Blood Star and an assortment of
punctuated moles, heavy with the lack of
touch. Notice how our areolas sleep like
nesting snail, warm mollusk body cupped by
bra. I wish this were a love letter or a
Nerudaesque ode but you are thirty years of
slanted rain. I write this braless,
without blouse and warmed by the dapple of
white sun bleaching the skin.

No, I lie to you breasts. I sit twisted as
always into this vise grip of black satin,
underwire sneering. The padding, the lift,
the lace and trellis of the pinched
breasts. This embarrassingly expensive
bra.

Understand that I hoped for you before I
knew what you were. In my embryo sleep of
dark matter and inner space, my
phantasmagoric fever, I sought you. First
for my mother's, and her already having cut
them from her chest, there was nothing left
for me.

And then for my own to rise like swelling
tides, like a labored moon and tethered
star. I courted the both of you. With the
wistful mirror gazes of adolescence. The
kneading of the tart nipple, the pull, the
stretch of skin. The bemoaning vigilance
that my body should open into symphony at
last.

And in the anger of spit I lashed at you. I
despised you like a father.

When you finally rose like a dusty bread
know that I never treated you like a spring
break calamity. When you sat dripping with
unused milk I mourned. When you slept
dreamless I let you rest. When you became
hardened soured apples I let you live.
When you drooped like eyelids I let you be
photographed. When you pushed against
another woman's body I let you sing. When
you agreed to take a husband I vowed we
should always be free.

To my first fleshly children who grew
despite me, I owe you something holy,
reverent. I owe you an apology.

Thought Woman

Thought woman created tortillas and flesh
like *masa* –
and perhaps she thought of violence
too. But, I will never know.

She thought of the sex of me,
all apple and dew.
Stitched a burlap body, brown of course
and blew sand into it.
This to be the me of me.

My insides *tierra* and just a drop of
moisture.

She took four long ropes of her hair.
Onyx like
Moctezuma's eyes and threaded the burlap
girl/boy body.

She named me desert.
She named me *una Esperanza*
de las Estrellas. She named me *Xilonen*.

Thought Woman sang me into this world –
to let me cry, to bleed,
give babies to this land,
invoke dream stories,
to inscribe the world with
my something.

My something is bone song.
is holler woman.
is thinfinger

and toes the hue of a waterless dirt.

When the sun woke I was young –
closer to the earth and hair to my waist.

By the midwinter of day –
I had peeled a baby from my womb, shorn
my scalp and grew rivers on my belly.

When the inevitable ink of night comes,
I will unbind my stitches, let
the sand run back home

Give back
this hair to
Thought Woman
so she may daughter
someone new

Kissy Kissy

~for the Young Feminist at the Playground

His mother gifted him the name Robert
meaning bright flame and keeper of fire
We just called him Bubba –
eloquence certainly not the average sixth-
grader's finest trait

a skinny boy like a live wire and
skin the color of ten melted
caramels atop a warm television set

He owned a head full of ink black curls,
kinky and coiled
tight as the tiny fingers I once saw etched
into a Japanese woodblock print
The Great Wave Off Kanagawa –

He liked me sure enough – called me
his woman, my sixth-grade hips
but only a slight jump rope
tremor beneath my yellow picture day dress.

It was the season for distraction
trapezoids and hypotenuse angles
like knees bent
an upside down photo booth face
from the monkey bars
all toothy smile and desert dry hair

the air tinkled with the silver bells
of the *paleta* truck that
slowly circled round and

round our playground
like an eager shark

Bubba asked me to meet him
during second recess behind
the kissing tree
and I would have if only
just to see the amber flame of his eyes
lashes long and spider soft
curled upward like a girl

He waited with his entourage of
kickballers and sixth-grade romantics
It was the historic kiss that never was

The cottonwood was afloat that day
seed like muted firefly or snow
or furry white boats that coasted and
caught the breeze to tickle my nose

I was perfecting the cherry bomb
from the top rung of the jungle gym

Twirling miles and miles above
earth and then leaping like
fireball into the air – Queen of my own
Queendom for those last precious
fourteen minutes and forty-two seconds

forty-one seconds
forty seconds
of second recess

I was not the kisser of boys.
Nobody's hipless woman.

No make-believe wife
playing house behind the Maple tree.

Kissy Kissy McKisser Face!
In front of a squealing
pre-pubescent congregation,
the scent of stale lunch milk
rolling in hot waves
from their collective breath

Instead I was song in motion – leopard
print trapeze artist all glitter and glow
"The Most Marvelous Magnanimous
Lady Gymnast" there ever lived!

I was Barbette the Enigma,
El Nino Farini and The Flying Zedoras
Lily Leitzel of the Leamy Ladies,
wings taped to my back
clad in off-the-rack discount
knock-off high-top Converse

The undisputed star prima-donna
of the triple somersault,
Thank you VERY MUCH
your, Majesty!

⊥ was Cherry Bomb,
Spider Monkey Dash
Kick Flip Forward
Flop and Scratch
Mark Dismount

but
          most

```
TRIUMPHANTLY
                    and
      GLORIOUSLY
              of
                    all
I was free.
I was free.
I was free.
```

The Daughter

The evening that I notice my girl is
changing, sprouting
with hair into womanhood,
I see crisp lines like
small black lightning erupt from the
inverted spoon of her left armpit.

The heat presses against the window
a boiling summer monsoon and she
is a sweat tangle
fast asleep on my side of the bed.

The butter pallor of the reading lamp
permeates every corner of my bedroom
illuminating the salt beads that
congregate at her temples.

I sit awhile and watch her.

One arm is thrown above her head as if
she aims to catch a pop
fly in her unconsciousness.
The other arm pressed to the small bell of
her rib cage.
The arm is a small branch a bird might
perch upon.

The chest rises and falls
like a doughy bread.

This is my life's purpose,
monitor the breath, the hair
that takes to her legs like

a brush fire across California
summer hills. To move the
lithe body from one bed to another.
To notice the faint shadow like a dusty
charcoal above the lip.

I know her body like I know my own.

I am prepared to be prepared
for this shift,
this inevitable change of
the cosmological order of her being.
I am her ordained keeper of body.

And it is when I know
that I must let go
that the real dying will begin

That mother and daughter diploid cells
will have truly separated into their
own acts of insular creation.

That I must step away and watch
from the light house that all old
mothers retire.

Now, I hold the golden meiosis
of her body close
this sweaty sleeping girl who almost
slips through my arms and walk from
the buttery light and into the greatness
of the long dark hallway.

I never hurt nobody but myself and that's nobody's business but my own.

-Billie Holiday

The Mother

I haven't written a poem in your likeness
for some time. I tried. I took
the broom and beat the cobwebs.

Lit one hissing cigarette after
hissing cigarette. Let a dish fall to
the floor, a porcelain scream.
I let the quiet shattering happen
but could not eek it out.

Then I thought of this. You the young
mother, a knotted belt at your waist,
slim and attractive in photos. Your
teeth gleaming and straight
like a string of pearls.

You hosted one birthday party in honor
of me my whole life. I was four years young
and it was a California Easter Sunday.
The kind of Sunday people move
to the West Coast for.

You drew caricatures of rabbits and
fashioned yellow tufts of baby ducks.
Dressed me in my best cut-off jeans
and plaited my hair.
Posed me in front of the cake, the cousins,

the wrapped gifts.

Picture after picture
reveals that I was happy.

Mother, you were perfect as a plum then.
Slicing the cake. A knife
just a knife in your hand
and nothing more.

I am ten years older than you then.
A whole decade and more of misdirected men
have come and gone for me, a daughter
of my own. Many birthdays since
that I care less to remember.

And it took me this long to notice
the one thing missing from those
Easter photos that long ago day.

The father.

Wednesday's Wife

I am Wednesday's wife
and you arrive fresh from
the train with your crooked
smile and smell of the city
on your clothes and in your hair.

I have been playing good
woman all day –

all day soaping laundry,
boiling tea leaves and even scrubbing
the shit from the dogs' kennels –

all in the name of the wooly
musk of your maleness. I didn't
find your lost set of car keys
Love and my disappointment
was a dangerous sadness.

Today, I cried when I murdered
five blue bottle flies with the hot pink
swatter we bought from the thrift store
their oily bodies smeared across the
kitchen window.

How could I mourn such pitiless creatures?
Such insignificant blood?

What new meekness is me?
Where is my flaming bra?

The delightful shuddering
fault line that you provoke,

with a single finger
a sideways glance
stirs me to a maddening surrender.

I am Wednesday's wife, Thursday's martyr,
a penny-pinching Friday mother.

I greet you at the door
like a loaf of starch white bread
like a commercial for laundry detergent
or Stouffer's Triple Cheese Casserole.

I search your eyes for the weather.
It is five o' clock everywhere in the
world.

If you were a woman
perhaps I would
take up no such issues
with my easy submission

but that was an old courage
that failed me long ago
and the tall masculinity of
you is a familiar robe

we are the newfound
apprentices to our shared silences
 – waiting

I could curl up like a lapdog
and let you watch me die
let you crush me with your
oh-so-larger-than-life love

I could slip the knife from
the woodblock and hold it
to my own neck to save
you the time

instead I shave the carrots
with it

insidious in its sharpness
laboring beneath my deft fingers
dicing potatoes, cutting chicken
from bone, paring away the
gristle and fat and meat of life

You settle into your evening
your shoulders a big chair
your comfortable love.

You eye me like a high-ball.

In the kitchen the water
is coming to a frantic boil.

Pots spit an urgent steam
from the side of their
metallic lips, murmuring
something
something
indecipherable.

I lean recklessly
over the open range,
the heat of it enflaming
the skin over my breasts
ear close as to not miss
a single sound of these

individual flames
each pan sizzling
a new sing-song
that sounds like this:

Dinner is almost done, dear.
Dinner is almost
done.

Diana the Huntress

They say the number four bus enjoyed
a certain reputation
its tires swaggering down a hilly road
pockmarked by sage brush
loose in the axle like a man
with too many beers under his belt

the fear exhaled from the women's nostrils
fueled the trek –
a hot mist moist with the tang of terror
bus windows fogged by morning vapor
opaque and rheumy long after the women
had vacated their seats

I took a pistol and placed a bullet
into the bus driver's temple
easily I deposited it there
the sun made a wistful track along the
soot-covered sky
and the *maquilas* shut their
metal doors against the day
El Paso glittered like a City of Gold from
the other side of the border
a muffled silence settled into
all of our bones

at the arrival of the next dawn
I took a second bullet
silver as the a single bead from the rosary
my mother wore around her neck
pregnant in the womb of the chamber
the bullet spat with *quickfire* and lodged

into the second man's brain

again no pity,
no sorrow-colored remorse
only the old number four tossed
like a tin can
I walked away and did not run from the
dead man bloated and gray faced
his back and arms laced with the scarred
scratches made by the women
who had not got away

The newspapers jabbered like angry bees
and the AP wire was alive with the
electricity of my name

Diana the Huntress
and I fear no moon, Lady of Wild Creatures
La Cazadora worshipped by the womanly
workforce
of Juarez

My sisters are frightened mares

Some might say I will perish in hell with
the rest of them
the men – adept at removing women's faces
removing their breasts like too-soon petals
the milk of their skin, the floating
flotsam
peeled beneath the killer's knife

They like to leave behind bite marks on the
buttocks

They like to leave behind dead babies
cradled within eviscerated wombs

Decomposed flesh resting
inside decomposed flesh

And should I burn in the seventh layer
it is of no consequence to me
place me in hell and I will kill them all
again

should my skin peel from my bones
incinerated by the heat of the oldest sin
I will always think it worth it
judge me Creator for I fear no moon

no man
no law
no lawlessness
no rampage

I only ever wanted to fashion birds with
these hands
I only ever wanted soft righteousness not a
countryside
riddled with the husks of dead raped women

They were like wild mustangs,
the dark-eyed girls, cuckolded
shepherded to the slaughter;
knees like young colts,
necks bared and naked breasts
an offering to the swine

All of their holes raped,
looted and left to spoil

the assembly plants are swollen
with the limbs of women
the dirt is caked with their blood

We are not our fathers' daughters
Our husbands' wives
We are our mothers' weeping

Don't you know
you who wrought me
wrenched me from my terrible anger
dug out from the shell of my sleep with a
dirty fingernail
my rebirth whispered
upon the dying lips of women
one last jewel of blood dropped to the
floor

reaping
sowing

beseeching
vengeance

one fine golden
and glorious
day?

About the Author

Recently named one of 30 Poets in their 30's to watch by MUZZLE magazine, Jessica Helen Lopez is a nationally recognized award-winning slam poet, and holds the title of 2012 and 2014 Women of the World (WOW) City of ABQ Champion.

She's also a member of the Macondo Foundation. Founded by Sandra Cisneros, it is an association of socially engaged writers united to advance creativity, foster generosity, and honor community.

Her first collection of poetry, *Always Messing With Them Boys* (West End Press, 2011) made the Southwest Book of the Year reading list and was also awarded the Zia Book Award presented by NM Women Press. She is the founder of La Palabra – The Word is a Woman collective created for and by women and gender-identified women. Lopez is a Ted Talk speaker alum.

You may find some of Lopez's work at these sites –LaPalabra.abqnorthwest.com, thebakerypoetry.com, and asusjournal.org.

Her work has been anthologized in A Bigger Boat: The Unlikely Success of the Albuquerque Slam Scene (UNM Press), Earth Ships: A New Mecca Poetry Collection (NM Book Award Finalist), Tandem Lit Slam (San Francisco), Adobe Walls, Malpais Review, SLAB Literary Magazine and the upcoming Courage Anthology: Daring Poems for Gutsy Girls (Write Bloody Press).

Gratitude

I am grateful for my friends, *familia* and poetry cheerleaders. Thanks to all those who, time and time again, attend poetry slams. Without our community we are nothing.

Special thanks to my best buddies Katrina, Zachary, Mariah, Brooke and ABQ Slams. My husband tambien. Also, to my pre-teen daughter who consistently challenges my definition of *feminista* and the reconciliation of the word CUNT amongst others. I am grateful for that too.

Thank goddess for our collective La Palabra – The Word is a Woman. I am always overjoyed to work with such talented, fierce and fiery women/gender-identified women and allies. As usual, you are all my favorite hooligans.

photo credit Gina Marselle 2010

Made in the USA
Middletown, DE
20 February 2018